A PORTRAIT OF
LANCASTER

Jon Sparks

HALSGROVE

First published in Great Britain in 2005

British Library Cataloguing-in-Publication Data
A CIP record for this title is available from the British Library

ISBN 1 84114 452 5

HALSGROVE
Halsgrove House
Lower Moor Way
Tiverton, Devon EX16 6SS
Tel: 01884 243242
Fax: 01884 243325
email: sales@halsgrove.com
website: www.halsgrove.com

Printed and bound by D'Auria Industrie Grafiche Spa, Italy

Introduction

Lancaster has been good to me, both as a place to grow up and live in, and more specifically, as a place to photograph. I had my first exhibition here in 1990, and soon afterwards, I began producing local greetings cards and postcards. It wouldn't be much fun photographing the same place for over fifteen years unless that place was really worth photographing, and Lancaster certainly is. In fact it has always seemed to me to offer unusually rich pickings for the photographer.

It's not just that Lancaster has some fine buildings, although it certainly does as I hope the following pages will demonstrate. There's more to it than individual buildings; there is something on a bigger scale, something about the basic geography of the place that sets it apart from many other historic towns and cities.

That underlying geography is in essence very simple: two hills and a river. Above all I think it's the way the River Lune curls around Castle Hill that creates so many different angles and perspectives. It also makes it possible to move quickly from narrow streets into green spaces, and onto hilltops where vast prospects open out. These extend not just over the rooftops of the town but out to rolling fields and on to the high heather moors of Bowland, the crumpled Lakeland skyline, and the ever-changing vastness of Morecambe Bay.

Lancaster has also been lucky in being spared the worst excesses of inappropriate development. Most of its modern buildings, like the Marketgate Centre, are on a reasonable scale and in sympathy with their surroundings. Above all, they don't dominate the skylines which are such a feature of Lancaster views.

For a city of its size, Lancaster also has an exceptionally vibrant cultural life. This must owe much to the presence of the university, which stands on a ridge just outside the town, separate but not isolated. And Lancaster is full of people who came to study and never wanted to leave.

Lancaster is also fortunate in the fact that it still has edges. It hasn't been swallowed up by urban sprawl. True, to the west it does join on to Morecambe, but even here the river creates some physical and psychological space. To south and east, in particular, you don't have to go far at all before you emerge into open country, and pretty nice country at that. In fact there are places where livestock grazes within a kilometre of the castle. Some excellent walking and cycling paths mean that a visitor arriving at Lancaster station can get out into the country without ever having to travel along a road.

It's a bit like having your cake and eating it; living in a place that you like but also knowing that you can get out of it easily and quickly, and that there are lots of destinations to choose from. I've illustrated a few of these towards the end of the book. All of them are accessible by local bus, an easy bike ride, or a walk of no more than a few hours. Lancaster sits comfortably between coast and hills: Clougha Pike, in the Forest of Bowland Area of Outstanding Natural Beauty, is so close that people regularly drive out and run up and down it in their lunch hour. Breezy Morecambe, which boasts the best sunsets in the world (and I'm not arguing), is even closer.

Of course Lancaster is changing, and I have tried to avoid using any photograph that is obviously out of date. This has meant that some sentimental favourites haven't made it. To try and keep up with developments, some images in the book were shot in the last few days before the deadline. Change will continue, and so it should. One can only hope that it will be done with due sensitivity to the character of the place. I do believe it's somewhere special and I hope this book helps to show why.

Jon Sparks

Statue on the Ashton Memorial
The Ashton Memorial stands on Lancaster's highest hill. On clear days it gives tremendous views
over the city, Morecambe and its bay and the Lake District Fells beyond. I'd been granted special access to a
higher balcony at the base of the dome, where three statues represent Science (seen here), Art and Industry.

Fountain, the Ashton Memorial
There is a lot of fine detailing on the Memorial,
like this stone lion, one of three around its base.

The Ashton Memorial and Lakeland Fells

The Ashton Memorial is usually thought of as a great viewpoint towards the Lakeland Fells. From the Langthwaite ridge a little further east, it becomes part of that view. The fells on the skyline are above the Duddon valley and there's just a glimpse of Morecambe Bay in the middle distance. The glass roof of the Butterfly House is also visible.

Parapet, the Ashton Memorial
This detail of the parapet caught my eye while I was taking a
series of shots including the one on page 5. The low-angled
evening light picked out these fossils in the Portland stone.

Opposite: **The Ashton Memorial in springtime**
The Ashton Memorial is a familiar sight to travellers on the M6 motorway,
though many of them do not know what it is. It was built for Lord Ashton,
formerly 'Lile Jimmy' Williamson, who made a fortune from linoleum and
oilcloth. In the late nineteenth century, he was the undisputed overlord
of the town. The white Portland stone building was completed in 1909
and stood above all as a memorial to Ashton's wife.

The Ashton Memorial, falling snow
The Ashton Memorial is the centrepiece of Williamson Park, whose other attractions include
the tropical Butterfly House, as well as promenade theatre productions in the summer.

Opposite: **Steps of the Ashton Memorial**
The Memorial's sloping site gives space for this grand flight of steps, which aren't
of Portland stone like the memorial itself but of a light-coloured granite.

Trees in Williamson Park
Williamson Park
occupies a site which
was previously a quarry;
much of the city is
built from stone
excavated here.

Butterfly House
Next to the memorial stands the Orangery, now better known as the Butterfly House.
I've photographed here several times, and it always seems to be chilly outside, which means
waiting anything up to half an hour for condensation to clear from cameras and lenses.
And then there's the problem of persuading the butterflies to sit still…

The Ashton Memorial and Moon from Skerton Bridge
Sadly, it seems necessary to stress that this is not in any way a 'trick' shot: there is no
double exposure or digital trickery involved; just being in the right place at the right time.
The shot also shows what a dominating position the Memorial occupies above the city.

Opposite: **The Ashton Memorial**
I took advantage of bleachers erected for one of the annual Duke's Theatre promenade productions to get a more
elevated viewpoint than is usually possible. This puts the Memorial and its grand steps in a better perspective.

Maple, Williamson Park
A wet day did nothing to dull the colours of this bush; if anything it made them even more vibrant.

Gates of Williamson Park
Evening light was perfectly angled to catch the park gates
(this is the Wyresdale Road entrance).

Golgotha village

The cottages are charming, but the name has sinister overtones, as it was in this area that executions took place for several centuries, most famously those of some of the Pendle Witches. It's said that the condemned were allowed a last drink at the Golden Lion inn, on the way from the Castle to what was then an isolated hilltop site outside the town.

Dallas Road
Lancaster has many good
nineteenth-century houses, these
on Dallas Road being fairly typical.
But I must admit it was the reflections
on the wet pavement that made
the shot interesting for me.

19

Clayton Bridge
This stretch of the canal is directly below St Peter's Cathedral, which will appear later in the book.

Opposite: **Frozen canal and St Peter's Cathedral**
The Lancaster Canal follows an elevated course to the east of the city centre. The building in
the middle distance is Moor Lane Mill, one of a number of old mills along the canal which have found
a new lease of life, in this case as the headquarters of well-known sports footwear company
Reebok UK. The spire belongs to St Peter's Roman Catholic Cathedral.

Castle Park
I wish Castle Park always looked like this – sunny and free of cars. It's already a fine
urban space, but freed from traffic it could be something very special indeed.

Opposite: **The Priory Steps**
There are several ways to approach the Priory Church but if you come from
the town centre this is the natural way, and it seems to me to be the best.

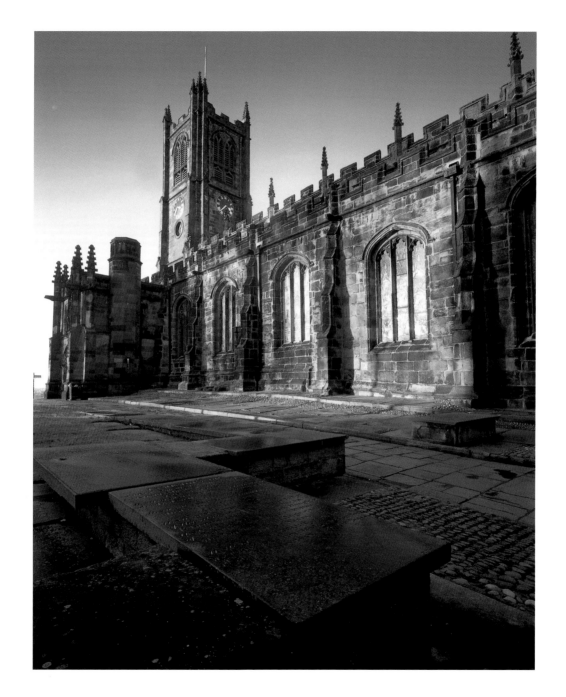

Choirstalls, the Priory Church
These carved oak choirstalls, dating from the fourteenth century,
are probably the finest feature of the interior of the Priory Church.
Only Winchester and Rochester cathedrals have older examples.

Opposite: **The Priory Church**
The Priory – full name the Church of the Blessed Mary of Lancaster – is one of the
finest parish churches in the county. Its origins are Norman, and there was almost
certainly a Saxon church on the site before that, but most of the visible structure dates
from the late fourteenth and early fifteenth centuries.

The Shire Hall
Much of Lancaster Castle is used as a prison. For as long as I can remember there has been talk of this coming to an end and the whole of the Castle being opened to the public, but it remains a distant prospect. However, there is plenty of interest in the part you can see, notably the Shire Hall. Towards the left of the picture is part of the display of over 600 heraldic shields, including the arms of monarchs, Constables of the Castle, and High Sheriffs of Lancashire.

Interior, the Priory Church
The Priory Church underwent
extensive restoration to mark the
900th anniversary of the Norman
foundation in 1094. It is considered
a very fine example of the
English Perpendicular style.

Spring, Castle Park
Most of the houses around the
Castle date from the eighteenth
century, when Lancaster enjoyed
a period of great prosperity based
on its Atlantic trade.

Opposite:
Beacon, the Priory churchyard
This beacon was first lit in 1988 to
mark the 400th anniversary of the
Spanish Armada, and has played its
part in other festivals since then.

28

Castle Hill and the Ashton Memorial from Salt Ayre

A long-lens view from some distance away, which appears to compress the distance between Castle Hill and the higher ridge on which the Ashton Memorial stands; the whole of the city centre lies in that hidden dip.

Opposite: **The Priory Church, snow**

I think this shot shows that the Priory is not just a beautiful building but has some grand spaces around it. Yet there has recently been a proposal – which almost beggars belief – to turn much of this land into a car-park.

Corner of St Mary's Parade
St Mary's Parade lies just below the Castle. It's intriguing to think that
the street sign is probably the most modern feature in the photograph.

The Ashton Memorial from Castle Park
I think this shot emphasises the much greater height of the hill on which the Memorial stands.
You might wonder why this commanding position wasn't chosen for the Castle, and the main
reason was that Castle Hill was close to an important river crossing.

Houses on Castle Park
These houses face almost due north and it was late on a
summer evening when I found them so beautifully lit.

Opposite: **Covell Cross and Judges' Lodgings.**
Standing on the site of a much more ancient cross, Covell Cross is named for Thomas Covell,
one of the judges in the notorious Pendle Witch Trials. The house behind, reckoned to be
Lancaster's oldest, was built for Covell but is invariably known as Judges' Lodgings; it was
used until 1975 to accommodate judges travelling to the Assizes at Lancaster Castle.

Looking up to the Castle
Judges' Lodgings appears again on the right of
this picture. Two of the towers in the curtain wall
of the Castle can be seen and behind them just
a small part of the massive Norman keep.

St Mary's Parade
Most of the houses that surround the Castle are quite grand, but those on St Mary's Parade are on a more modest scale.

The Priory Church, detail
The porch in the foreground dates from 1903 but the main walls behind are fifteenth century.

Shire Hall, snow
The Shire Hall is a relatively late addition to the Castle – it was completed in 1798 –
and it does look a bit like an annexe, though a very grand one.

Castle Hill from Highfield
Highfield, a little below Williamson Park, gives a good perspective from which to appreciate the true proportions of Lancaster Castle and in particular the central keep. The industrial buildings of White Lund emerge from the mist behind the Castle, and beyond them are Morecambe and Morecambe Bay.

Opposite: **John o'Gaunt's Gate from the King's Arms**
John O'Gaunt's Gate is the best-known feature of Lancaster Castle. John was the father of King Henry IV, in whose reign the the gateway was built. Ironically, apart from collecting the vast revenues of the Duchy of Lancaster, John O'Gaunt had very little connection with the city: some authorities state that he only spent nine days here. The gable-end and slate roof in the foreground belong to the building which now houses Lancaster's busy Tourist Information Centre.

Visitors to the Priory Church
I'd been allowed to climb to the top of the Priory Tower, which gave me some great aerial views, but my favourite shot was this quick snap of a school party visiting the church.

42

St Mary's Gate
St Mary's Gate lies below the Priory Steps, and leads on down to Church Street. On the right of the shot is the side of the Judges' Lodgings.

Window in the Priory Church
It was, of course, the light falling through
the stained glass onto the 500-year-old
stonework that drew my eye.

The Priory Church
This is one of the classic viewpoints for the Priory. The tower is relatively recent, dating from 1755.

Doorway, St Mary's Gate
This fine house stands at the top of St Mary's
Gate and didn't quite squeeze into the
shot on page 43.

Portico of Judges' Lodgings

Visitors to Judges' Lodgings pass under this portico. Inside they can admire
the interior of the house and also enjoy its collection of furniture by the famous
Lancaster firm of Gillow, while on the top floor is a Museum of Childhood.

Castle Hill
In the foreground is the entrance to the Cottage Museum, which occupies a small house dating from 1739, later divided into two, and now furnished in the style of the early nineteenth century.

Opposite:
The Storey Institute
Thomas Storey was a major industrial proprietor in Victorian Lancaster, though never quite as famous as Williamson/Ashton. However he also left an enduring legacy to the town in the Institute which bears his name and now houses the town's principal public art gallery.

Evening light, St Mary's Gate
These houses spend much of their time in the massive shadow of the Castle,
but mornings and summer evenings show them in better light.

Opposite: **The Shire Hall**
Framed by the trees in the Priory churchyard, the Shire Hall
almost seems to stand on its own.

Amphitheatre, the Priory churchyard
Old grave slabs provide the tiers of seating in the amphitheatre, which is used
from time to time for performances during festivals.

Vicarage Field
Raking light picks out intriguing lumps and bumps in the field; some limited archaeological excavation has taken place but there is still much to learn about the site, which is known to have been occupied in Roman times.

Lunchtime below the Castle
On a summer's day, this is a fine spot to take a break.

The City Museum, St Peter's Cathedral and the Ashton Memorial from Castle Hill
I'm a sucker for misty shots and this is an old favourite.

Reflections, River Lune and St George's Quay
The mid-eighteenth century was Lancaster's real heyday; for a few glorious years it
was Britain's second port. Many warehouses survive, though long since converted to other
uses, mostly residential. Care has been taken to ensure that modern additions harmonise
with the established buildings, and the Quay retains a strongly Georgian aspect.

Opposite: **Train and Castle Hill**
Lancaster is on the West Coast Main Line and you can get to London in under three
hours and – much more important – you can get back to Lancaster equally quickly.

St George's Quay, the Millennium Bridge and St Peter's Cathedral
Lancaster's newest bridge stands in almost the same place as the earliest known crossing of the Lune, which has been used since Roman times.

Opposite:
Walker on the Lune Aqueduct
The Lancaster Canal crosses the Lune by the impressive Lune Aqueduct. The hill on the horizon is Clougha Pike, in the Forest of Bowland Area of Outstanding Natural Beauty.

River Lune from Carlisle Bridge
Carlisle Bridge carries the main railway line across the river and there's a footbridge
alongside, which gives this view upstream towards the city centre.

Opposite: **The Customs House and the Priory Church**
The centrepiece of St George's Quay is the beautiful Customs House, designed by Richard
Gillow and dating from 1764. Today it houses a fascinating Maritime Museum.

Cyclist on the Millennium Bridge
It has to be said that the Millennium Bridge has its critics, but to me it is far finer than either Greyhound Bridge, just upstream, or Carlisle Bridge further down. The fact that it is dedicated to pedestrians and cyclists is another point in its favour.

Rowers on River Lune
I was being bounced around in a small inflatable dinghy and more than half the shots from this session
were ruined by camera-shake. The rowers were students from Lancaster Royal Grammar School.

Pillars, the Customs House
The Customs House was designed by Richard
Gillow, of the famous furniture making family.
The pillars are notable because they aren't in
sections: each is a single block of stone

The Lune Aqueduct
The Lune Aqueduct, designed by John Rennie, is a powerful structure but less well-known than other local landmarks, probably because there is no good view of it from a road.

The Lune Aqueduct
The aqueduct was completed in 1797 to carry the Lancaster Canal over the river
on its way to Kendal, but so great was the expense that no money remained for another
aqueduct at Preston, which would have linked the canal to the rest of the network.

Opposite: **St George's Quay and the Priory Church, winter**
It was a chilly morning and there wasn't really enough snow for
Christmas-card type shots, but the light was perfect.

**Skerton Bridge and
The Ashton Memorial**
Skerton Bridge was built in 1783,
replacing an older structure which
stood near the location of the
modern Millennium Bridge.

Opposite:
Crossing Skerton Bridge
For bridge aficionados, Skerton Bridge
is of great historical significance, being
the first bridge of its size anywhere in
the country to have a level roadway.

The Millennium Bridge and Castle Hill
Castle Hill rises on the skyline and St George's Quay extends off to the right, while to the left
are some of the new buildings around Fleet Square. This major development, still under
construction as this book went to press, will include housing, shops and cafés.

Cyclist and River Lune

Alert readers will have spotted that this picture predates the Millennium Bridge. It shows a section of the cycle route (a former railway line) which leads to Morecambe, but until the Millennium Bridge was completed there was no continuation into the centre of Lancaster; you either mixed in with the traffic or carried your bike up several flights of steps to cross Carlisle Bridge. Nowadays cycling is usually the quickest way to travel between Lancaster and Morecambe.

The Millennium Bridge and Greyhound Bridge
Greyhound Bridge was built in 1848 to carry the North Western Railway
(the 'Little North Western') line to Morecambe. When the railway closed in 1965,
the bridge was converted to carry road traffic.

Opposite: **Skerton Bridge and Castle Hill**
Essential ingredients for this shot included a high tide, lack of wind,
sun setting behind the Castle – which it only does around the winter
solstice – and a break in the traffic crossing Skerton Bridge.

Crossing the Lune Aqueduct
I was grateful to the builders of
the aqueduct for providing such
broad parapets, as I had to stand
on one to get this shot, and there's
quite a drop: the canal is about
20 metres above the river.

St George's Quay
Despite the obvious temptations of the pub, it's that crooked house which really catches the eye.

The Customs House
Elegance is the word again: this shot from across the river shows off the classical proportions of the Customs House.

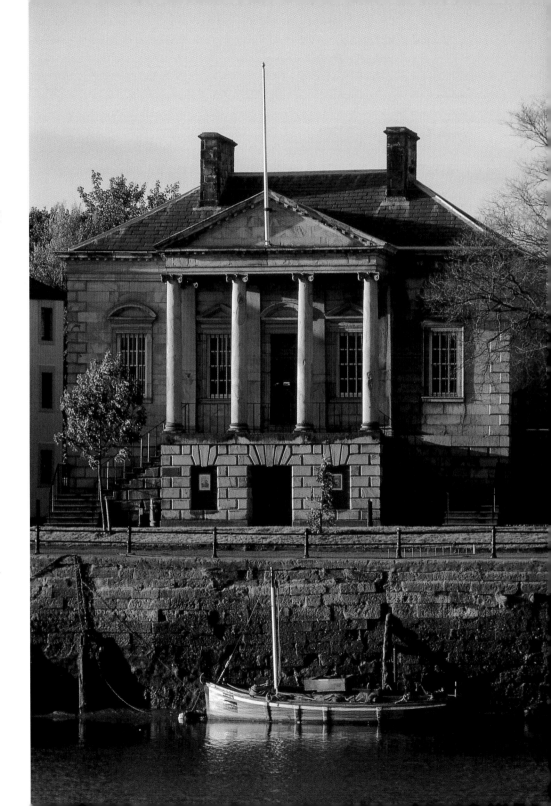

Opposite:
Skerton Bridge
Bridge engineers may be impressed by the level roadway, but it's the sheer elegance of the bridge that I admire.

Roofs, Castle Hill
I liked the haphazard nature of the different surfaces, but I suspect the shot
would not have worked as well if that lamp had been straight.

Festival in Market Square
Castles and memorials may be the glamorous
locations, but Market Square is the real heart
of Lancaster; although it has to be said it
doesn't usually look quite like this.

Below the Victoria Monument, Dalton Square
This gathering of eminent Victorians is on the plinth of the Victoria
Monument in Dalton Square – there are more on the other three sides.

Opposite: **Market entrance**
Possibly the most traumatic day in Lancaster's history within my lifetime was when the old
Market was destroyed by fire. Market traders carried on business under a temporary roof for
a few years before a new market finally opened as part of the Marketgate development.

**The Victoria Monument
and the Town Hall**
A summer's evening
in Dalton Square.

Opposite:
The Ashton Memorial from Freehold
The Freehold area lies on the rising
ground east of the town centre. Warm
evening light glows on the Portland
stone of the memorial and the local
sandstone of the houses.

83

Lancaster from Davidson Street
Real 'Christmas card' conditions like this are rare, and getting rarer. An early start was needed to make the most of it.

The King's Arms Hotel

It is officially the Royal King's Arms Hotel, but to locals it's just The King's Arms, and the name over the entrance agrees. According to the hotel's website, it lies 'in the shadow of Lancaster Castle' and late on a summer evening it might just be literally true. Its upper floors certainly offer great views of the castle, as seen on page 40.

Castle Hill and the Coniston Fells

An earlier but very similar shot, used on greetings cards and a local calendar, attracted a lot of attention and many people thought it was some kind of trick photograph. But the only trick involved was finding the right spot to shoot from. I keep hoping that one of the doubters will put money on it. The distant fells – almost 40 kilometres away – are Dow Crag on the left and Coniston Old Man on the right, with Scafell appearing between them, above the church tower.

Opposite: **Lancaster Canal and St Peter's Cathedral**

St Peter's Roman Catholic Cathedral was built between 1857 and 1859 to the design of Edward Paley, a local architect best known as part of the Paley and Austin partnership, which was responsible for many of the finest churches and other buildings in north-west England. The spire is about 75 metres (240 feet) tall.

The Water Witch
The Water Witch, alongside the canal, is one of Lancaster's most popular pubs,
especially when the weather is warm enough for sitting outside.

St John's church
St John's church is a product of Lancaster's
Georgian prosperity, built in 1754-55, with
a tower added thirty years later.

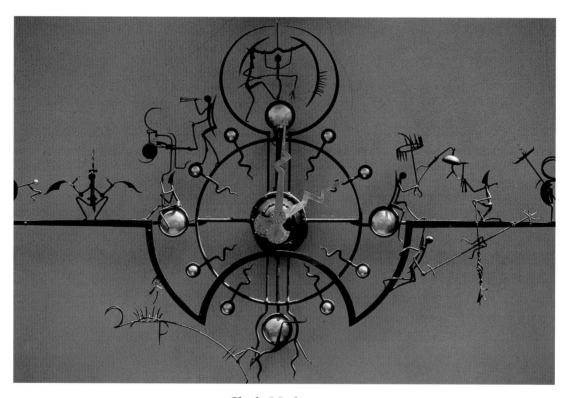

Clock, Marketgate
There is a good deal of attractive detailing in the new
Marketgate centre, but pride of place goes to this clock.

Lancaster Canal and White Cross
The mill complex of White Cross
has been resurrected as home to
many small businesses. The artfully
restored buildings provide office and
light manufacturing space, as well
as housing the Adult College, the
White Cross pub, and the local
Granada TV studios.

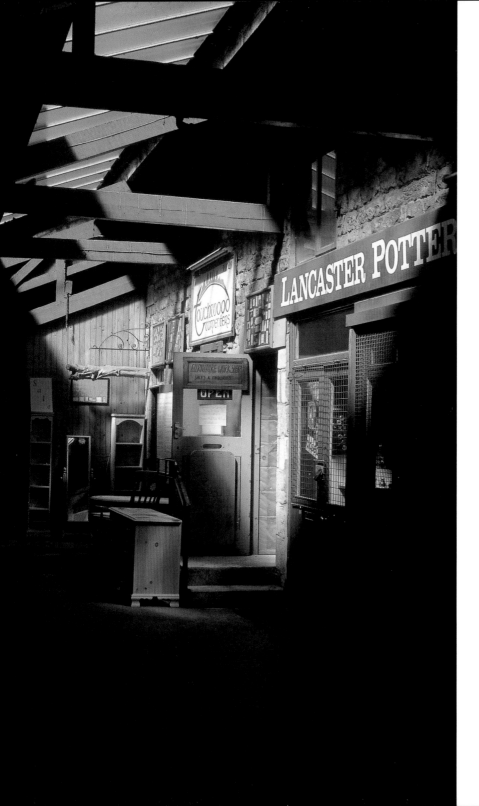

The Covered Yard
This is one of the quirky corners that you can find in most old towns. It opens off the busy King Street and I'm sure many people drive past every day without realising that the yard exists.

New Street
I liked the light on the wet surfaces
here. The rocking horse above
Lawson's toy-shop shows up
well too; to many people it is
still 'the rocking-horse shop'.

Lancaster Canal below Bath Mill Estate
The Bath Mill Estate, as the name suggests, stands on another old mill site,
and won a national civic award for its sensitive redevelopment.

Opposite: **Town Hall from White Cross**
Just a glimpse of the Town Hall clock from within the White Cross complex.

Penny's Almshouses
The almshouses, named after William Penny,
a former Mayor of Lancaster, were built in 1720,
to provide accommodation for 'twelve poor men'
of the city, and are still inhabited today.

Penny Street
William Penny is also commemorated in Penny Street, one of Lancaster's main shopping streets.

Town Hall from Dalton Square, evening
The Town Hall opened in 1909, having cost £155,000 – probably at least £5 million in today's
values. The Victoria Monument which faces it was unveiled a couple of years earlier.

Opposite: **Market Square and Museum**
Market Square has been the heart of Lancaster for hundreds of years.
The 'new' Town Hall, seen in the picture above, replaced the Georgian structure
seen in the background here, which is now home to the City Museum.

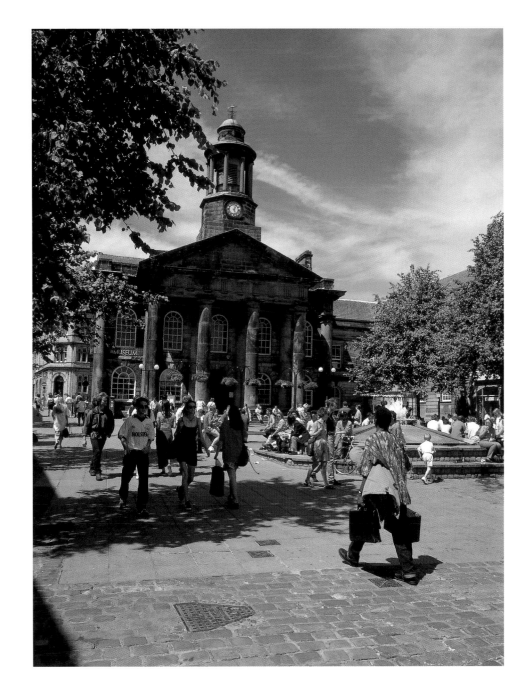

Passage, Marketgate
This passageway links the Marketgate centre and Common Garden Street. It's in constant use but I wanted to show it without people so that the murals of sheep and shepherds could be seen.

Interior, St John's church
The interior of St John's hasn't changed much since it was first completed; notable
Georgian features include the box pews and the painted texts around the chancel walls.

Pestle and mortar

In the days before many people could read, shop and pub signs employed common symbols. Some are preserved in museums but in-situ survivals are few and far between. The apothecary's pestle and mortar still stand above a modern pharmacy.

Mill Hall
It was the play of light that attracted me, but you can also appreciate the use of good local stone in the building.

Castle Hill, the Ashton Memorial and Bowland Fells
The telephoto lens does compress the apparent distances, but even so this shot demonstrates how close Lancaster is to the fells. The summit of Clougha Pike, seen to the left of the church tower, is about 8km (5 miles) away as the crow flies.

Opposite: **The Royal Albert**
The Royal Albert Institution, as it was originally called, was established in 1868-73 'for the care, education and training of feeble-minded children and young persons belonging to the seven northern counties'. Having long since outlived its usefulness for its original purpose, it has found a new lease of life as a school for Muslim girls.

St Peter's Cathedral and Primrose
Looking from Castle Hill in evening
light, past the Cathedral, to the ranks
of rooftops in Primrose. The trees
beyond are part of Williamson Park.

Opposite:
Rooftops, Primrose
This view too shows the closeness
of open country to the city. The Lune
estuary is in the middle distance with
Heysham on the ridge beyond. For
years the estuary has been threatened
by a proposed new road but
fortunately this prospect currently
seems to be receding.

Walking to school through Ryelands Park

In the days when I also produced local Christmas cards, I used to rush out at
every hint of snow, but as often as not it was wasted effort. I was just about to give up
and go home when I spotted this shot. I just knew I'd be able to use it one day!

Opposite: **Lancaster Moor Hospital, snow**

Lancaster Moor Hospital served the area for over 180 years but is no longer in clinical use and
its future is uncertain. To the right of the tower is Black Combe, beyond Morecambe Bay.

Lancaster Canal, White Cross and St Peter's Cathedral
This was a largely cloudy evening but the sun broke through briefly.
I just had time to set up the tripod and take a couple of shots.

Opposite: **Burrow Beck and cycle-path**
This is right on the southern edge of the city. The cycle-path continues
through fields to Lancaster University. On a couple of occasions I have
seen a kingfisher along this stretch of the beck.

Fireworks over Castle Hill
A major fireworks display on Lancaster Castle Hill, on the Saturday nearest to November 5, is now an established part of the local calendar, and I have photographed it from various vantage points. On this occasion I had been given access to a rooftop in the Royal Lancaster Infirmary.

Sedan chair racing
This is something you don't see every day, and probably not even every year, but sedan chair races have been a feature of a number of Georgian Legacy Festivals held in Lancaster. It's hard work for the carriers and must be unnerving for the passenger.

Castle Hill from Lucy Brook
A strip of farmland pushes close to the heart of the city; sheep
and cattle regularly graze within a kilometre of the Castle.

Evening, Lancaster Canal

It may not be Oxford or Cambridge, but punting along the canal on a balmy summer's evening still seems like a very pleasant occupation. But it seems it didn't catch on: I don't think anyone is currently offering punts for hire.

Sheep, Burrow Heights
Burrow Heights is a low ridge just south of the city. Lancaster University rises behind.

Opposite: **Bandstand, Ryelands Park**
A very different aspect to Ryelands Park from the winter scene on page 109.

Ducks on the canal
These mallard ducks happened to live where the canal runs through open country just south of town, but they could have been almost anywhere along its length.

Opposite: **Field of Hope, St Martin's College**
St Martin's College began as an Anglican College of Education, but now offers a wide range of degree courses. It originally occupied the Bowerham Barracks but soon outgrew these. I think it's a fair bet that its overly-prominent tower block would not get planning permission today. The Field of Hope is one of many around the country planted in aid of Marie Curie Cancer Care

Towpath and White Cross
Once the canal was Lancaster's commercial artery; today both waterway
and towpath are given over almost entirely to recreational uses.

Opposite: **Castle Hill from above Springfield Bridge**
Springfield Bridge, off Aldcliffe Road, leads to a footpath climbing over Haverbreaks Hill.
I suspect this view is unfamiliar to most local people except those who actually live close by.

Canal boat and St Peter's Cathedral
The Lancaster Canal was hampered throughout its working life because there was no link to the rest of the canal network. Ironically, there now is, as the Millennium Link in Preston enables boats to reach the Leeds and Liverpool Canal.

Opposite:
Daffodils, Lancaster University
Lancaster University was inaugurated in 1964 and construction at Bailrigg, just south of the city, began in 1965. Today it is established as a leading university, recently rated among the top 12 in the UK for research and in the top 20 for teaching.

**Lancaster University
and Ward's Stone**
The original white-topped buildings
of the University were supposedly
intended to create the impression of
an Italian hill-town. I'm not sure this
was ever hugely successful and many
of the more recent buildings have
abandoned this convention anyway.
Bowland Tower is part of the original
central core while the Ruskin Library
in front is much more recent. In
the distance is Ward's Stone, highest
of the Bowland Fells.

Infolab 21, Lancaster University

This is a very recent addition, officially opened in February 2005. It is dedicated to research and development in information and communication technology. Reflected in the glass are the residential buildings of Pendle College.

Eric Morecambe statue, Morecambe Promenade
One of the country's best-loved comedians, Eric
Morecambe was born Eric Bartholomew but took his
stage name from his birthplace. The statue, by
Graham Ibbeson, was unveiled by the Queen in July
1999. Eric Morecambe was also a dedicated bird-watcher,
so his statue carries a pair of binoculars.

The Midland Hotel, Morecambe

This, it must be admitted, is not a current picture. The Midland Hotel is a unique example of the Art Deco style but has been neglected for decades, and those hoping to see it restored to former glory have seen several false dawns. However, at time of writing it does finally seem that plans to restore it will go ahead.

Fence of birds, Morecambe Promenade
Morecambe Bay is a very important area for bird life, and this is commemorated
by the TERN project, which has created a range of public art, including games,
mazes and tongue-twisters, along the Promenade.

Wave, Morecambe
I got wet feet taking this shot, and so did the tripod, but it seemed a small price to pay.

Evening, Morecambe Bay
Morecambe Bay achieved national prominence for all the wrong reasons in
February 2004 following the deaths of 23 Chinese cockle-pickers: a tragic reminder
that this vast tidal expanse can be as dangerous as it is beautiful.

Opposite: **Heysham Head and Morecambe Bay**
These 'stone coffins' on the sandstone cliffs of Heysham head have been the subject
of many theories and legends, but they are much too small to be adult graves and
seem wrongly proportioned even for children. The mystery remains. Close by is a
ruined chapel, reputedly marking the spot where St Patrick first set foot in England.

Ice, Crook O'Lune
Crook O'Lune is about 6km (4 miles) upstream from Lancaster. Here the River Lune makes a sharp bend where it breaks through a natural rock barrier. The Crook is a popular spot, with excellent access including a cycleway from Lancaster.

Opposite: **Riders, Hest Bank Sands**
Hest Bank is just up the coast from Morecambe, and at low tide a large area of firm sand is exposed, on to which it is generally safe to venture as long as you know when the tide will come back in – which it does, proverbially, 'faster than a horse can gallop'.

Anglers, River Lune
Above Crook O'Lune, the Lune valley opens out into a broad pastoral landscape.
The river is highly regarded for both salmon and coarse fishing.

Opposite: **Sunderland from Tithebarn Hill**
The small village of Sunderland, more commonly called Sunderland Point, stands near the mouth
of the River Lune. On the horizon (right) is a ship heading out from the nearby Port of Heysham.

Above Crook O'Lune
This view is looking downstream. Lancaster itself is hidden by the wooded ridge (Knots Wood) on the skyline

Opposite: **Bluebells, Quernmore**
The Quernmore valley is literally just over the hill from Lancaster but remains largely pastoral. The name is locally pronounced 'Kwormer', and is derived from 'quern', (pronounced as it is spelt), meaning a millstone. Millstone grit occurs on Clougha Pike, which rises above the valley, and abandoned querns can still be found in a few places on its flanks.

Station Clock, Carnforth
A five-minute train ride from Lancaster, Carnforth station famously figured in the 1945 film *Brief Encounter*, starring Celia Johnson and Trevor Howard. A railway station is central to the story, and Carnforth's curved platforms provided ideal camera angles. The distinctive clock also played a significant role. After many years of decrepitude, the station has now been restored to something like its former glory.

Opposite:
Baines Crag and Ward's Stone
Baines Crag is only a few kilometres from Lancaster, on the edge of the Forest of Bowland Area of Outstanding Natural Beauty. The new 'right to roam' legislation has opened up vast areas of these fells previously off limits to walkers.

Lion, Dalton Square
This lion is one of four at the feet of Queen
Victoria's statue in Dalton Square. It strikes me
that it has a curiously contemplative look – or
was it just the summer evening light?

Cygnets, Lancaster Canal
Even in the city, but much more so as it breaks out into open country, the Lancaster Canal
is an important corridor for wildlife as well as humans. These young mute swans
were seen near Galgate, a few kilometres to the south of Lancaster.

Crocuses, Heysham
The twelfth-century church of St Peter at Heysham is partly sheltered by the rocks of
Heysham Head. The church is noted for its Norman features and for its 'hogback' tombstones,
thought to be of Viking origin, but above all for this display of crocuses in February.

Panorama from Williamson Park
Williamson Park offers a superb panorama on any clear day, but only in high summer can you watch the sun set behind the Lakeland Fells, beyond the sweep of Morecambe Bay.

Sunrise, from Castle Hill
This shot is taken from the top of the Priory Steps, and the curtain wall of the Castle is on the right.
The sun is rising directly behind the tower of St Martin's College and the city's other great landmarks –
the Ashton Memorial, St Peter's Cathedral and the Town Hall – are all in their familiar places.